I0458476

# Questions for My Dad to Share His Life

# Questions for My Dad to Share His Life

A Guided Journal with Prompts, Reflections and Family Activities to Preserve Your Father's Legacy

Aria Capri Publishing

The original purchaser of this book has permission to reproduce the pages of this book for personal use only. No other parts of this publication may be reproduced in whole or in part, shared with others, stored in a retrieval system, digitized, or transmitted in any form without written permission from the publisher.

Copyright 2021, Aria Capri Publishing Group (Aria Capri International Inc). All rights reserved.

Authors:
Aria Capri Publishing Group
Mauricio Vasquez

First Printing: April 2025

ISBN 978-1-998729-25-8 (Electronic book)
ISBN 978-1-998729-24-1 (Hardcover book)
ISBN 978-1-998729-23-4 (Paperback)

Dear Valued Customer,

As a family-owned business, your review means the world to us.

It only takes a moment—just scan the QR code to leave your feedback. Your review helps others discover this book and create more love and connection in their own families.

Thank you for your support!

Mauricio

---

**Want to Capture Mom's Story Too?**

Celebrate your mother's life and legacy with the companion journal, Questions for My Mom to Share Her Life.

Scan the QR code to get your copy and preserve her memories for generations to come.

Because both stories deserve to be told. 🩶

# Empower Your Connections:
## Discover More Tools to Strengthen Relationships.
### Scan the QR Code Today

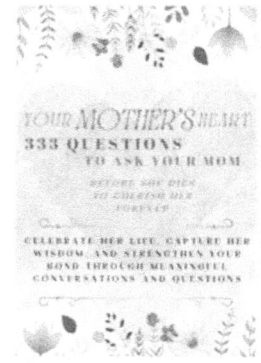 

# Table of Contents

# Introduction

This journal was created for you—fathers of all types, both biological and those who stepped into the role—to capture the important moments that have shaped your life.

Your stories and wisdom can only be passed down to future generations if you take the time to share them.

This book is designed to help you write down your memories, stories, and thoughts, turning this guided journal into a precious keepsake to share with your children, loved ones, and future generations.

The thoughtful questions make it easy to record everything from your childhood memories and important life lessons to your hopes for the future.

When completed, this book will help your children and grandchildren better understand your family's history and roots.

Most importantly, this journal will tell your unique story. It's how your family will learn about who you really are, beyond just being "Dad," and will create a meaningful connection with them. This lasting keepsake gives you the chance to inspire future generations with your experiences, accomplishments, and the wisdom you've gained throughout your life.

# Making This Journal Your Own

This journal is your personal space for reflection—there's no rulebook to follow.

Make this experience work for you. Jump between questions that catch your interest, circle back to others when memories surface, or methodically work from page to page. The path you take is entirely yours to choose.

Every question is simply an invitation. Some might spark detailed stories, while others might not connect with your experience at all. Feel free to change a question to better match your journey.

The most valuable entries often come when you let your thoughts flow naturally. Don't worry about crafting perfect sentences or organizing your thoughts;—just let your authentic memories and feelings guide your pen. Your family will treasure your genuine voice more than polished prose.

Bring your stories to life with vivid details. Rather than writing "we went to the beach," specify "we built sandcastles at Lighthouse Point on that sweltering July afternoon in 1982." Instead of "I drove my first car," share how "my hands trembled with excitement on the wheel of that rusted blue Ford Mustang with the cracked leather seats." These specifics transform memories into experiences your readers can almost see and feel.

This journey through your memories deserves time and space. Consider setting aside a regular moment—perhaps Sunday mornings with coffee or quiet weekday evenings—to revisit and record your stories. Many fathers find it takes several months to complete their journal, allowing memories to unfold naturally.

For a different approach, consider having someone interview you. A child or grandchild might enjoy asking these questions while recording your spoken responses, capturing your voice, laughter, and the natural rhythm of conversation.

The notes pages at the end of each section offer extra room when memories overflow, space for photos that complement your stories, or spots to answer additional questions from our website.

Remember—this process isn't about creating a perfect document, but about sharing the unique story that only you can tell. Enjoy the journey of rediscovery as you create this lasting gift for your family.

**To enrich your journaling journey, we've created a special bonus:** a 30-Day Family Bonding Challenge filled with simple, meaningful activities to enjoy with your loved ones.

Scan the QR code to download your free printable and create even more memories— together.

# Who I Am & Moments That Matter

# About Me

MY FULL NAME:

BIRTHDAY:

| BIRTHPLACE: | EYE COLOR: |
|---|---|
| HEIGHT: | HAIR COLOR: |

ANY SPECIAL
TRAITS:

ATTACH YOUR PHOTO HERE:

# A Snapshot of My Time

TODAY'S DATE:

| | |
|---|---|
| POPULATION OF MY CITY: | POPULATION OF MY COUNTRY: |
| PRESIDENT OR PRIME MINISTER OF MY COUNTRY: | WORLD POPULATION: |

## COMMON COSTS AT THIS MOMENT IN TIME:

| | |
|---|---|
| A TANK OF GAS: | A BASIC CAR WASH: |
| A CUP OF COFFEE: | A 6-PACK OF BEER OR SOFT DRINKS: |
| A FAMILY MEAL: | A MOVIE TICKET: |
| A PAIR OF WORK OR RUNNING SHOES: | A HAIRCUT: |
| POSTAGE STAMP | MONTHLY RENT/ MORTGAGE PAYMENT |
| A TOOL OR HARDWARE ITEM I USE: | A BASIC SMARTPHONE OR MOBILE PLAN: |

ADD A HEADLINE OR FRONT PAGE FROM
TODAY'S NEWS TO CAPTURE THE WORLD AROUND YOU:

# My Earliest Memories

Is there a story behind your name? Were you named after someone special in your family?

_____

_____

_____

_____

_____

_____

Have you always liked your name? Did you ever want a different one?

_____

_____

_____

_____

_____

_____

If you could have picked your own name, what would it be and why?

_____

_____

_____

_____

_____

_____

How old were your parents when you were born? Do you think their age affected how they raised you?

_____

_____

_____

_____

_____

_____

What have you been told about the day you were born? Was there anything unusual or special about it?

_____

_____

_____

_____

_____

_____

Were you a healthy baby or did you have any health problems? How did this affect your early years?

_____

_____

_____

_____

_____

_____

What baby stories about you did your parents like to tell? Which ones made them smile the most?

_____

_____

_____

_____

_____

_____

_____

What's your earliest memory? How did it make you feel?

_____

_____

_____

_____

_____

_____

_____

How was your upbringing different from how your parents were raised? What traditions did your family keep or change?

_____

_____

_____

_____

_____

_____

_____

What do you know about your first home? What memories do you
have of it?

_____

_____

_____

_____

_____

_____

Which of your personality traits come from your mother or father? How
have these traits shaped your life?

_____

_____

_____

_____

_____

_____

_____

# Notes

# Notes

# My Childhood Years

What special toys or objects did you treasure as a child? How did you
get them and what memorie s do they bring back?

_____

_____

_____

_____

_____

_____

What games did you love to play as a child? How did you play
differently when alone versus with friends?

_____

_____

_____

_____

_____

_____

What were you afraid of as a child? How did you deal with these fears,
and did anyone help you?

_____

_____

_____

_____

_____

_____

What smells, sounds, or tastes instantly remind you of your
childhood? What memories come back when you experience these
things?

_____

_____

_____

_____

_____

_____

Where did you spend most of your time playing as a child? How did
these places make you feel?

_____

_____

_____

_____

_____

_____

Did you have your own bedroom growing up? How did having your
own space or sharing with others affect you?

_____

_____

_____

_____

_____

_____

What did you like or dislike about where you grew up? How did your neighborhood shape who you became?

_____

_____

_____

_____

_____

_____

What were mealtimes like in your family? Did you have any special rules or traditions?

_____

_____

_____

_____

_____

_____

What do you remember about your childhood kitchen? What sights, sounds, and smells stand out in your memory?

_____

_____

_____

_____

_____

_____

What foods did you hate as a child? Do you still dislike them? Are there any funny stories about your food preferences?

_____

_____

_____

_____

_____

_____

What chores were you responsible for as a child? How did you feel about doing them?"

_____

_____

_____

_____

_____

_____

Besides your parents, who were important adults in your childhood? How did they influence you?"

_____

_____

_____

_____

_____

_____

What activities did you enjoy doing with your parents? What feelings come back when you remember these times?

_____

_____

_____

_____

_____

_____

How was your relationship with each of your parents different? What shaped these relationships and how have they changed?

_____

_____

_____

_____

_____

_____

What challenges did your family face? Were you sheltered from these problems or involved in solving them?

_____

_____

_____

_____

_____

_____

Did you get an allowance as a child? What did you spend it on or save for?

_____

_____

_____

_____

_____

_____

Did your family have enough money when you were growing up? What did you learn about money during your childhood?

_____

_____

_____

_____

_____

_____

How did you handle peer pressure as a child? How did you balance fitting in with staying true to yourself?

_____

_____

_____

_____

_____

_____

What comments from teachers do you still remember? How did their words affect how you saw yourself?

_____

_____

_____

_____

_____

_____

What subject do you wish had been taught in school? How might it have changed your life path?

_____

_____

_____

_____

_____

_____

What were your favorite subjects in school? How did these interests help shape who you became?

_____

_____

_____

_____

_____

_____

What activities did you participate in outside of regular classes? How did sports, music, or clubs help you grow?

_____

_____

_____

_____

_____

_____

What sports teams did you cheer for as a child? What memories do you have of watching games with others?

_____

_____

_____

_____

_____

_____

What memories from high school are still clear in your mind? What feelings come back when you think about those teenage years?

_____

_____

_____

_____

_____

_____

What achievement from your childhood or teen years are you most
proud of? How did this success affect your confidence?

_____

_____

_____

_____

_____

_____

What were summers like when school was out? What activities or
traditions made these breaks special?

_____

_____

_____

_____

_____

_____

Who were your closest friends growing up? How have these
friendships changed over time, and do you still keep in touch?

_____

_____

_____

_____

_____

_____

Did you have friends your parents didn't approve of? How did you
handle the situation when they didn't like your friends?

_____

_____

_____

_____

_____

_____

How were you disciplined when you got in trouble? How did you
respond when you were being punished?

_____

_____

_____

_____

_____

_____

Did your family take vacations? What do you remember about these
trips away from home?

_____

_____

_____

_____

_____

_____

What special days did your family celebrate each year? What traditions made these occasions meaningful?

_____

_____

_____

_____

_____

_____

What's one celebration from your childhood that really stands out? Why was this event so special?

_____

_____

_____

_____

_____

_____

Would you say you had a happy childhood? What parts brought you joy or difficulties?

_____

_____

_____

_____

_____

_____

What advice would you give to your teenage self today? What wisdom
have you gained that would have helped you then?

_____

_____

_____

_____

_____

_____

What important life lessons about money would you like to pass on to
your children and grandchildren?

_____

_____

_____

_____

_____

_____

# Notes

# Notes

# How I Spent My Time

How did your career develop over time? Who or what influenced your job choices, and how did chance play a part?

_____
_____
_____
_____
_____
_____

What did you do after high school - college, trade school, military, or work? How did these experiences shape you?

_____
_____
_____
_____
_____
_____

What important moments do you remember from your early adult years? Which experiences, relationships, or accomplishments from this time still matter to you?

_____
_____
_____
_____
_____
_____

Looking back at your choices after high school, are there any you'd change? What have you learned about the paths you took or didn't take?

_____

_____

_____

_____

_____

_____

What advice about education and personal growth would you give to your grandchildren? What principles about learning do you think will always be important?

_____

_____

_____

_____

_____

_____

What was your first paying job? How did earning your own money change how you thought about work and value?

_____

_____

_____

_____

_____

_____

How did you get your first job? What circumstances, connections, or personal efforts helped you fird it?

_____

_____

_____

_____

_____

_____

What jobs have you had throughout your life? Which ones helped you advance, which took you off track, and which ur expectedly changed your direction?

_____

_____

_____

_____

_____

_____

What job did you enjoy most? What made it so satisfying - the people, the purpose, or the opportunities it ofered?

_____

_____

_____

_____

_____

_____

Where did you first live after moving out of your parents' home? Who did you live with, and how did this first independent home shape who you became?

_____

_____

_____

_____

_____

_____

What's the most valuable lesson you learned in school that has helped you in real life? How has this knowledge or skill supported you throughout your life?

_____

_____

_____

_____

_____

_____

Who taught you how to drive? What do you remember about learning to drive that has stayed with you?

_____

_____

_____

_____

_____

_____

What pets have you had in your life? How did they affect you
emotionally, and what special memories do you have of them?

_____

_____

_____

_____

_____

_____

What hobbies or interests have you pursued outside of work? How did
you discover these activities, and how have they changed over time?

_____

_____

_____

_____

_____

_____

What activities bring you the most joy or satisfaction? How do these
favorite pastimes connect you to what's truly important to you?

_____

_____

_____

_____

_____

_____

# Notes

## My Family Connections

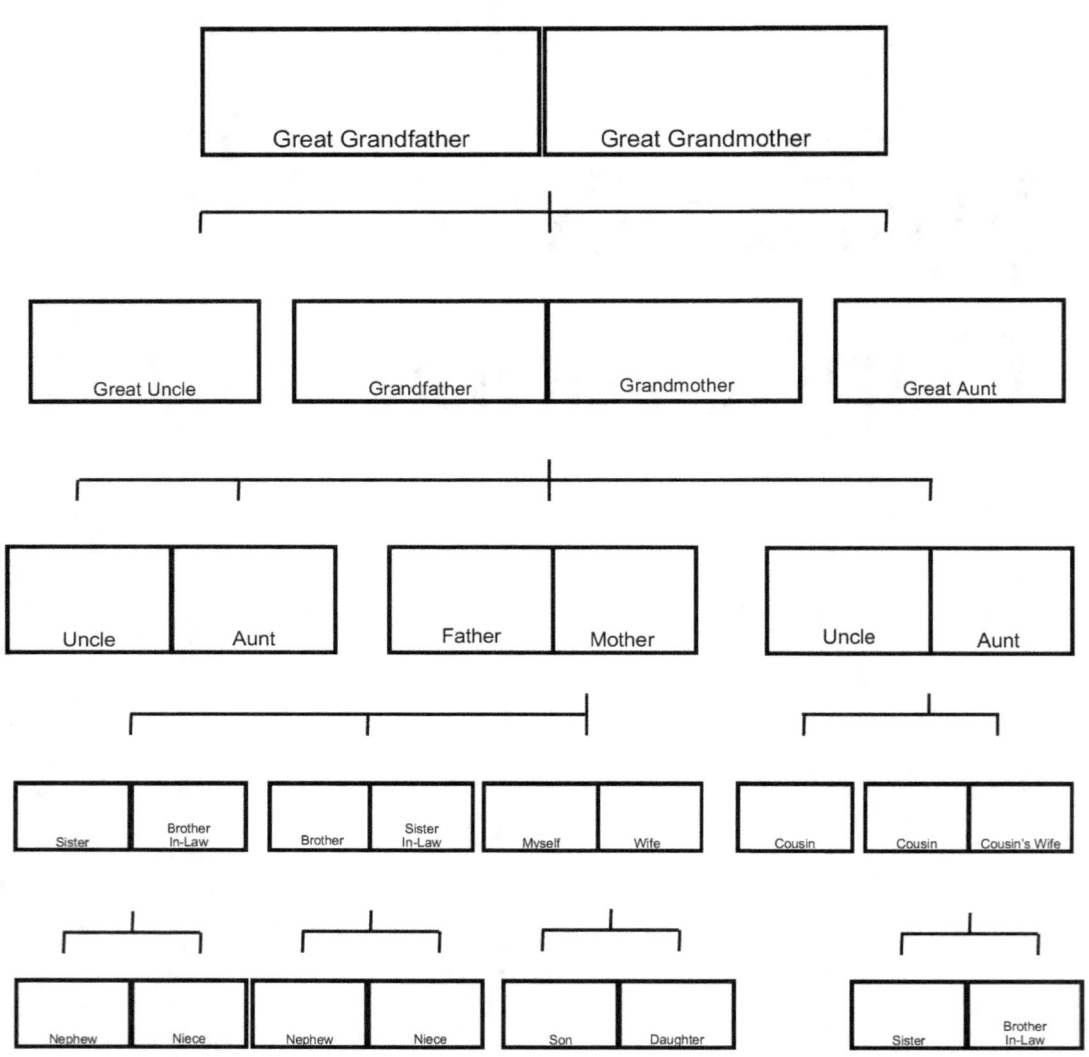

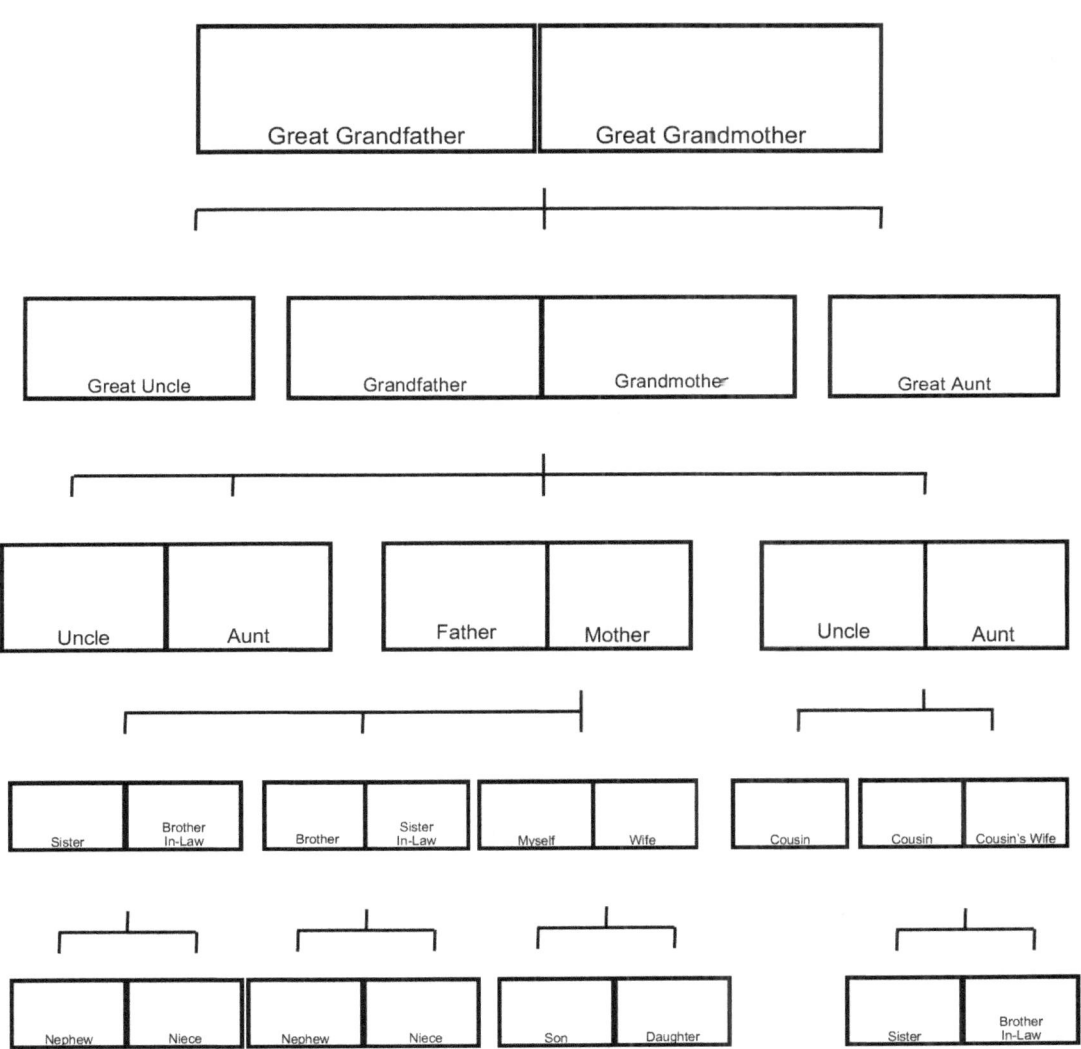

# Notes

---

# Relationships That Defined My Story

# About My Parents

FIRST NAME

FAMILY NAME

| BIRTH PLACE | DATE OF BIRTH |
|---|---|
| EYE COLOR | HAIR COLOR |

OCCUPATION

FIRST NAME

FAMILY NAME

| BIRTH PLACE | DATE OF BIRTH |
|---|---|
| EYE COLOR | HAIR COLOR |

OCCUPATION

How was your relationship with each of your parents when you were growing up? How has your relationship with them changed as you've become an adult, and what have you learned from these changes?"

What important lessons or values did you learn from each of your parents? How have these lessons or values continued to be important throughout your life?

_____
_____
_____
_____
_____
_____
_____
_____
_____
_____
_____
_____
_____
_____
_____
_____
_____
_____
_____
_____
_____
_____

# My Brothers and/or Sisters

FIRST NAME

FAMILY NAME

BIRTH PLACE

DATE OF BIRTH

EYE COLOR

HAIR COLOR

OCCUPATION

- - - - - - - - - - - - - - - - - - - - - - - - - - - - - - - - - - - - -

FIRST NAME

FAMILY NAME

BIRTH PLACE

DATE OF BIRTH

EYE COLOR

HAIR COLOR

OCCUPATION

- - - - - - - - - - - - - - - - - - - - - - - - - - - - - - - - - - - - -

FIRST NAME

FAMILY NAME

BIRTH PLACE

DATE OF BIRTH

EYE COLOR

HAIR COLOR

OCCUPATION

- - - - - - - - - - - - - - - - - - - - - - - - - - - - - - - - - - - - -

FIRST NAME

FAMILY NAME

BIRTH PLACE

DATE OF BIRTH

EYE COLOR

HAIR COLOR

OCCUPATION

What traits do you share with your siblings in looks, personality, or viewpoints? What similarities connect you, and what differences have led you on different paths?

_____

_____

_____

_____

_____

_____

_____

_____

_____

_____

_____

_____

_____

_____

_____

_____

_____

_____

_____

_____

_____

_____

_____

_____

_____

How would you describe your relationships with your siblings when you were children? How did getting along or not getting along affect both your shared childhood and who you each became?

_____

_____

_____

_____

_____

_____

_____

_____

_____

_____

How have your relationships with your siblings changed throughout your life? What important experiences or realizations have strengthened or changed these relationships as you've grown older?

_____

_____

_____

_____

_____

_____

_____

_____

_____

_____

# About my Grandparents

FIRST NAME

FAMILY NAME

BIRTH PLACE | DATE OF BIRTH

EYE COLOR | HAIR COLOR

OCCUPATION

- - - - - - - - - - - - - - - - - - - - - - - - - - - - - - - - - - - - - -

FIRST NAME

FAMILY NAME

BIRTH PLACE | DATE OF BIRTH

EYE COLOR | HAIR COLOR

OCCUPATION

- - - - - - - - - - - - - - - - - - - - - - - - - - - - - - - - - - - - - -

FIRST NAME

FAMILY NAME

BIRTH PLACE | DATE OF BIRTH

EYE COLOR | HAIR COLOR

OCCUPATION

- - - - - - - - - - - - - - - - - - - - - - - - - - - - - - - - - - - - - -

FIRST NAME

FAMILY NAME

BIRTH PLACE | DATE OF BIRTH

EYE COLOR | HAIR COLOR

OCCUPATION

What personality traits or characteristics run in your family across generations? Did any traits jump from your grandparents to you, skipping your parents? How have family traits changed as they passed down from grandparents to parents to you?"

How close were you with your grandparents? What special moments or memories with them still mean a lot to you today?

_____

_____

_____

_____

_____

_____

_____

_____

_____

_____

_____

_____

_____

_____

_____

_____

_____

_____

_____

_____

_____

_____

_____

_____

_____

What important lesson or advice did you learn from your grandparents? How has their wisdom or life experience continued to guide you even after they were gone?

_____
_____
_____
_____
_____
_____
_____
_____
_____
_____
_____
_____
_____
_____
_____
_____
_____
_____
_____
_____
_____
_____
_____
_____

# My Kids

FIRST NAME

FAMILY NAME

| BIRTH PLACE | DATE OF BIRTH |
|---|---|
| EYE COLOR | HAIR COLOR |

OCCUPATION

- - - - - - - - - - - - - - - - - - - - - - - - - - - - - - - - - - - - - - - - - -

FIRST NAME

FAMILY NAME

| BIRTH PLACE | DATE OF BIRTH |
|---|---|
| EYE COLOR | HAIR COLOR |

OCCUPATION

- - - - - - - - - - - - - - - - - - - - - - - - - - - - - - - - - - - - - - - - - -

FIRST NAME

FAMILY NAME

| BIRTH PLACE | DATE OF BIRTH |
|---|---|
| EYE COLOR | HAIR COLOR |

OCCUPATION

- - - - - - - - - - - - - - - - - - - - - - - - - - - - - - - - - - - - - - - - - -

FIRST NAME

FAMILY NAME

| BIRTH PLACE | DATE OF BIRTH |
|---|---|
| EYE COLOR | HAIR COLOR |

OCCUPATION

What qualities do you love and admire in each of your children? How have you seen these strengths develop over time, and can you share examples that show their special talents?

_____
_____
_____
_____
_____
_____
_____
_____
_____
_____
_____
_____
_____
_____
_____
_____
_____
_____
_____
_____
_____
_____
_____
_____

What are your hopes and dreams for your children and grandchildren? Beyond money and success, what values and experiences do you wish for them to have in their lives?

_____

_____

_____

_____

_____

_____

_____

_____

_____

_____

_____

_____

_____

_____

_____

_____

_____

_____

_____

_____

_____

_____

# Family

Which family members are most similar to you in personality or life path? Who are you closest to in your family, and how have these relationships changed over time?

_____
_____
_____
_____
_____
_____
_____
_____
_____
_____

What difficult times or conflicts has your family faced? How did these challenges change your understanding of forgiveness and family relationships?

_____
_____
_____
_____
_____
_____
_____
_____
_____

What interesting facts or history does your family have? Are there any family stories, heirlooms, or traditions that connect you to your larger family heritage?

# Friends

Who have been your closest friends in life? What experiences or moments with these friends have taught you what true friendship means?

_____

_____

_____

_____

_____

_____

_____

_____

_____

_____

Who is your oldest friend? How has your friendship changed over the years, and what has kept your connection strong for so long?

_____

_____

_____

_____

_____

_____

_____

_____

_____

_____

Has a friendship ever disappointed you or caused you pain? How did
you handle this difficult time, and what did you learn about
relationships from this experience?

_____

_____

_____

_____

_____

_____

_____

_____

_____

_____

Who do you turn to for advice? What was the best advice someone
gave you that really helped you or changed your path in life?

_____

_____

_____

_____

_____

_____

_____

_____

_____

_____

When has the fragility of human connection revealed itself within one of your valued friendships? How did you navigate this landscape of hurt or misunderstanding, and what insights about reconciliation or acceptance emerged from this experience?

_____

_____

_____

_____

_____

_____

_____

_____

_____

_____

Whose wisdom has served as a trusted lighthouse during your moments of uncertainty or decision? Which specific guidance from this trusted advisor proved particularly illuminating, perhaps altering your course in meaningful ways?

_____

_____

_____

_____

_____

_____

_____

_____

_____

# Relationships

How old were you when you went on your first real date? What happened on that date, and what do you remember most about it?

_____

_____

_____

_____

_____

_____

_____

_____

_____

_____

What stories from your dating life help explain your romantic history? What early crushes or breakups taught you important lessons about love?

_____

_____

_____

_____

_____

_____

_____

_____

_____

_____

How and when did you meet your partner? Was your early
relationship similar to or different from what your relationship
eventually became?

_____

_____

_____

_____

_____

_____

_____

_____

_____

_____

What qualities do you love most about your partner? How have you
seen these qualities show up in everyday life and during special
moments?

_____

_____

_____

_____

_____

_____

_____

_____

_____

_____

Tell me about your path from dating to marriage. What moments from your proposal and wedding day do you remember most clearly?

_____

_____

_____

_____

_____

_____

_____

_____

_____

_____

Based on your experience, what advice about love and relationships would you like to pass on to future generations?

_____

_____

_____

_____

_____

_____

_____

_____

_____

_____

# Notes

# Notes

●  ●  ●

# The Heart of Fatherhood

When did it first really hit you that you were going to be a dad? How did you feel when you realized your life was about to change?

_____

_____

_____

_____

_____

_____

_____

_____

_____

How did family and friends react when they found out you were going to be a father? Were there any reactions that surprised or touched you?

_____

_____

_____

_____

_____

_____

_____

_____

_____

How did becoming a dad change who you are and how you live?
What parts of yourself grew stronger or faded away when you became
a father?

_____

_____

_____

_____

_____

_____

_____

_____

_____

What parts of being a dad were most challenging for you? How did
you handle these challenges, and what did they teach you about
yourself?"

_____

_____

_____

_____

_____

_____

_____

_____

_____

How was being a father different from what you expected? What assumptions turned out to be wrong, and what unexpected joys or difficulties did you discover?

_____

_____

_____

_____

_____

_____

_____

_____

_____

How did your own childhood affect how you raised your children? Did you try to parent like your parents did, or did you consciously try to do things differently?

_____

_____

_____

_____

_____

_____

_____

_____

_____

What advice would you give to yourself as a new father? What do you wish you had known when you first became a dad?

_____

_____

_____

_____

_____

_____

_____

_____

_____

_____

Which age or stage of your children did you enjoy most as a father? Which stages were most challenging, and what did you learn from these different phases?

_____

_____

_____

_____

_____

_____

_____

_____

_____

_____

How is childhood today different from when you were growing up?
What changes do you think are good for kids today, and what
challenges do you wish they didn't have to face?

# Notes

# Notes

_____

●  ●  ●

# My Guiding Principles

What religious or spiritual beliefs were present in your childhood home? What traditions were you taught, and how have you kept, changed, or moved away from these beliefs as you've grown older?

_____

_____

_____

_____

_____

_____

_____

_____

_____

_____

How has your spiritual journey changed over the years? How have your beliefs about meaning in life or connection to something greater shifted through difficult times and important moments?

_____

_____

_____

_____

_____

_____

_____

_____

_____

_____

What do you love most about your country? How have your feelings about your national identity changed throughout your life and as the country itself has changed?

_____

_____

_____

_____

_____

_____

_____

_____

_____

What experiences or relationships have shaped your political views? Have your ideas about society and government stayed the same or changed as you've witnessed historical events?

_____

_____

_____

_____

_____

_____

_____

_____

_____

How were boys and girls expected to behave differently when you were growing up? How did you feel about these gender roles as a child, and how have your views changed over time?

_____

_____

_____

_____

_____

_____

_____

_____

_____

_____

Have changes in what you believe or understand led you to change your daily habits or choices? What new understandings have caused you to interact differently with the world?"

_____

_____

_____

_____

_____

_____

_____

_____

_____

_____

What charities or causes do you support? Why are these particular causes important to you, and do they connect to significant experiences in your life?

_____
_____
_____
_____
_____
_____
_____
_____
_____
_____

What core values have guided you throughout your life? What important truths or approaches to life would you most hope your children and grandchildren will carry forward?

_____
_____
_____
_____
_____
_____
_____
_____
_____
_____

# Notes

# Pages of Wisdom

How would you describe yourself? How has your understanding of
who you are changed as you've grown older?

_____

_____

_____

_____

_____

_____

_____

_____

_____

Is there anything in your family's medical history that your children and
grandchildren should know about? What advice about health would
you like to pass on?

_____

_____

_____

_____

_____

_____

_____

_____

_____

"What does success mean to you? Has this changed over time? Who do you consider successful, and why do you admire them?"

_____

_____

_____

_____

_____

_____

_____

_____

_____

_____

What has been your favorite age or stage in life? What made this time special or fulfilling?

_____

_____

_____

_____

_____

_____

_____

_____

_____

_____

Who has influenced you the most in your life? How did this person shape who you became and what you value?

_____

_____

_____

_____

_____

_____

_____

_____

_____

_____

Looking back, what do you wish you had made more time for? What experiences or activities deserved more attention?

_____

_____

_____

_____

_____

_____

_____

_____

_____

_____

What motivates you? What gives you purpose and keeps you going during both good and difficult times?

_____

_____

_____

_____

_____

_____

_____

_____

_____

What lessons about money would you like to pass on to your children and grandchildren? What have you learned from times of having enough and times of having too little?

_____

_____

_____

_____

_____

_____

_____

_____

_____

Besides raising your children, what do you consider your greatest accomplishment in life? What achievement, relationship, or overcoming of difficulties best shows who you really are?

_____

_____

_____

_____

_____

_____

_____

_____

_____

_____

Do you have any regrets about paths not taken in life? How have you come to terms with these regrets, or what do you still hope to resolve?

_____

_____

_____

_____

_____

_____

_____

_____

_____

_____

Have any disappointments or losses in your life surprisingly led to something good? Can you share examples of when something that seemed bad actually opened new doors?

_____

_____

_____

_____

_____

_____

_____

_____

_____

What difficult experiences from your lifetime would you want to protect future generations from? What advice would you give them about handling hard times?

_____

_____

_____

_____

_____

_____

_____

_____

_____

When was the most challenging time in your life? What helped you get through it, and how did it change you?

_____
_____
_____
_____
_____
_____
_____
_____
_____
_____

What was your scariest experience? How did you overcome your fear, and what did you learn from facing it?

_____
_____
_____
_____
_____
_____
_____
_____
_____
_____

What experiences have been so meaningful or joyful that you think
everyone should have them at least once in their life? Why?

---

---

---

---

---

---

---

---

---

---

What are the most amazing experiences you've had? Which ones
expanded your sense of what's possible and still inspire you today?

---

---

---

---

---

---

---

---

---

---

What is one trait about yourself you'd still like to improve? How has this quality affected your life journey?

_____

_____

_____

_____

_____

_____

_____

_____

_____

_____

What secrets have you discovered about living a fulfilling life? What principles or practices have helped you find genuine happiness?

_____

_____

_____

_____

_____

_____

_____

_____

_____

_____

What's the best advice anyone ever gave you? How did this advice
change your choices or outlook when you followed it?"

_____
_____
_____
_____
_____
_____
_____
_____
_____
_____

What would you want your great-grandchildren and future generations
to know about who you really are? Beyond basic facts, what would
you want them to understand about you as a person?

_____
_____
_____
_____
_____
_____
_____
_____
_____
_____

Based on your life experiences, what wisdom or advice would you share with others? What lessons from your journey might help guide those who come after you?

_____
_____
_____
_____
_____
_____
_____
_____
_____
_____

Which words of wisdom, offered perhaps at a pivotal moment or carried quietly through decades, have proven most illuminating on your path? How did this particular guidance transform your choices or perspective when you embraced it?"

_____
_____
_____
_____
_____
_____
_____
_____
_____
_____

If your voice could reach across time to the eyes and hearts of those who will carry your lineage forward, which truths about your essence would you most want to preserve? Beyond facts and dates, what understanding of who you truly were would you hope might echo through the generations yet unborn?

Which wisdom, distilled from your unique journey through joy and challenge, would you offer as lanterns to illuminate the paths of those who follow? What understandings, hard-won through lived experience, might serve as both compass and comfort for fellow travelers on life's road?

# Notes

# Quick Questions from My Life

What was your first word? How did people react when you said it?

_____

_____

_____

_____

_____

_____

_____

_____

_____

How old were you when you had your first kiss? How did it make you feel?

_____

_____

_____

_____

_____

_____

_____

_____

_____

When was the first time you fell in love? How did this experience
change how you saw yourself and others?

_____

_____

_____

_____

_____

_____

_____

_____

_____

What was the first movie you saw in a theater? How did this
experience affect you?

_____

_____

_____

_____

_____

_____

_____

_____

_____

When did you first try alcohol? What was happening at the time, and
what impression did it leave on you?

_____

_____

_____

_____

_____

_____

_____

_____

_____

_____

How old were you when you first drove a car? How did it feel to be
behind the wheel for the first time?

_____

_____

_____

_____

_____

_____

_____

_____

_____

_____

What was your first car? What was your relationship with this car, and did you give it a name?

_____

_____

_____

_____

_____

_____

_____

_____

_____

What was the first record, tape, or CD you bought with your own money? How did this music choice reflect who you were becoming?

_____

_____

_____

_____

_____

_____

_____

_____

_____

Who performed at the first concert you attended? How was seeing this
music live different from hearing it recorded?

_____
_____
_____
_____
_____
_____
_____
_____
_____

Where did you go on your first trip without your parents? How did this
independent travel experience change you?

_____
_____
_____
_____
_____
_____
_____
_____
_____

Where did you go for your first job interview? What hopes or worries
did you have as you applied for your first job?

_____

_____

_____

_____

_____

_____

_____

_____

_____

Who was the first person outside your family that you cooked a meal
for? Why did you want to prepare food for this person?

_____

_____

_____

_____

_____

_____

_____

_____

_____

When and where did you have your first car accident or fender bender? How did you handle this situation?

_____

_____

_____

_____

_____

_____

_____

_____

_____

_____

Where did you go on your first airplane flight? What was it like to fly for the first time?

_____

_____

_____

_____

_____

_____

_____

_____

_____

_____

# My Favorite Fives

What places you've visited have made the strongest impression on you? What locations do you still think about or dream about long after visiting them?

1. _____
2. _____
3. _____
4. _____
5. _____

What personal qualities or strengths have helped you most throughout your life? What aspects of your character do you value most in yourself as you've grown older?

1. _____
2. _____
3. _____
4. _____
5. _____

Who are your favorite musicians or bands? Which artists' music has meant the most to you during important times in your life?

1. _____
2. _____
3. _____
4. _____
5. _____

What advice would you give to your 16-year-old self? What wisdom do you wish you had known earlier that might have made your path easier?

1. _____
2. _____
3. _____
4. _____
5. _____

If you could have dinner with any famous people from history, who would you choose? Who would you most like to have a conversation with?

1. _____
2. _____
3. _____
4. _____
5. _____

Which frozen delights have most consistently brought you that singular pleasure unique to ice cream? What flavors carry the sweetest associations with particular moments or seasons of your life?"

1. _____
2. _____
3. _____
4. _____
5. _____

What are your favorite ice cream flavors? Do any flavors remind you
of special times or seasons in your life?

1.
2.
3.
4.
5.

What would you do if you won millions of dollars in the lottery? What
dreams would you fulfill if money were no object?

1.
2.
3.
4.
5.

What are the best gifts you've ever received? Which presents became
more than just objects and represented something special about your
relationship with the giver?

1.
2.
3.
4.
5.

# Things I Love

| | |
|---|---|
| COLOR | WEEKEND MEAL |
| CHILDHOOD TOY | MOVIE SNACK |
| BOOK | HOT DRINK |
| VACATION SPOT | SPORT TO WATCH |
| SEASON | TOOL OR GADGET |
| SUNDAY ROUTINE | CHILDHOOD GAME |
| CANDY | GO-TO COMFORT FOOD |
| TV SHOW | MOVIE |
| WAY TO RELAX | DRINK (ALCOHOLIC OR NOT) |
| PLACE I'VE BEEN | SOUND OR SONG |

# Quick Questions

Do you have a lucky number? Why is this number special to you?

_____

_____

_____

What type of weather do you like best? Why does this kind of weather suit your personality?

_____

_____

_____

Do you have a passport? What travels or border crossings has it helped you experience?

_____

_____

What food do you like when you're sick? Why is this food comforting when you don't feel well?

_____

_____

_____

Are you a morning person or a night person? How has this preference affected your daily routines?

_____

_____

_____

Do you buy lottery tickets or enjoy games of chance? Do you have any special rituals or patterns when playing these games?

_____

_____

_____

If you could instantly become an expert at something new, what would you choose? Why does this skill interest you?

_____

_____

_____

Who or what always makes you laugh? What people, memories, or situations can cheer you up even during difficult times?

_____

_____

_____

If you were granted three wishes, what would they be? What do these wishes tell us about what matters most to you?

_____

_____

_____

What simple pleasures do you enjoy most in life? What small,
everyday joys bring you happiness?

Have you ever won any competitions or contests? What achievements
are you particularly proud of?

What's the most expensive or extravagant thing you've ever bought?
Why did you decide to spend so much on this particular purchase?

What was the longest road trip you've ever taken? What interesting
things did you discover along the way?

What's the farthest you've ever traveled from home? How did this
distant journey change how you think about home?

Are you superstitious? Do you have any rituals or beliefs about luck, fate, or things that happen by chance?

_____

_____

_____

What is one of your worst habits? What behavior do you find difficult to change, even though you know you probably should?

_____

_____

_____

Do you prefer to be spontaneous or to plan things carefully? Which approach seems to work better for you in life?

_____

_____

_____

Have you ever broken any bones or had a serious injury? What happened and how did you recover?

_____

_____

_____

What do you tend to procrastinate about the most? Why do you think you put off these particular tasks?

_____

_____

_____

Do you believe in fate? How much of your life do you think was determined by chance versus your own choices?

_____

_____

_____

What do you think is a waste of money? How have your ideas about spending money changed through times when you had more or less of it?

_____

_____

_____

What is the most romantic thing anyone has ever done for you? Which loving gesture meant the most to you?

_____

_____

_____

Do you have a favorite saying or quote that guides your life? What wise words do you find yourself thinking about when facing difficult decisions?

_____

_____

_____

What makes a birthday special for you? How do you like to celebrate or reflect on your birthday each year?

_____

_____

_____

Have you met any famous people? How did these meetings happen?

_____

_____

_____

What would your ideal vacation be like? What things need to be included for you to truly enjoy and relax on a trip?

_____

_____

_____

Describe your dream home. Where would it be, what would it look like, and what special features would it have?

_____

_____

_____

List all the cities and towns where you've lived throughout your life. How did each place affect your life story?

_____

_____

_____

What are the top places you'd like to visit if money and time weren't issues? Which places in the world do you most want to experience?

_____

_____

_____

# Words for the
# Ones I Love

# Words for the Ones I Love

USE THIS SPACE TO SHARE A MESSAGE WITH SOMEONE YOU LOVE

# Words for the Ones I Love

# Words for the Ones I Love

# Words for the Ones I Love

# Words for the Ones I Love

_____
_____
_____
_____
_____
_____
_____
_____
_____
_____
_____
_____
_____
_____
_____
_____
_____
_____
_____
_____
_____
_____
_____
_____

www.ingramcontent.com/pod-product-compliance
Lightning Source LLC
Chambersburg PA
CBHW081719120626
46550CB00010B/3176